RUGBY SIMPLIFIED

HOW TO COACH 7'S RUGBY

WRITTEN BY

CHARLIE PURDON & IAN CAMPBELL-McGEACHY

Book design: Jasmine Vowels.

TABLE OF CONTENTS

1. SEVEN'S PHILOSOPHY

In the game of rugby sevens, the most important aim is to have possession of the actual ball. The reasoning behind this somewhat simple philosophy is based on the fact that the match is only 14 minutes long; therefore, it follows that the team that has possession of the ball ultimately controls the game. Maintaining possession of the ball requires a lot of skill as well as the ability to make quick, concise, and accurate decisions through numerous phases of attack.

The most important thing is to understand the difference between fun and enjoyment. Fun is what kids do.. Enjoyment is taking all the skills, values, and processes you've learnt and successfully implementing them."

- James Murphy

2. STRATEGY

Strategically speaking, the attackers must attempt to manipulate defenders by moving the ball into space, often from sideline to sideline until the defenders cannot physically defend anymore. Having the ability to distribute the ball quickly between players to areas of defensive vulnerability will ultimately tire defensive teams out, leading to lapses in concentration and space left open in or around the defensive line.

What you may have noticed so far is that 7's rugby consists of a lot of running and covering space, as the game is played on a regulation-size rugby field. 7's rugby players have to be extremely fit to keep up with the demand of the jobs tasked to them during a 7's match.

3. PLAYING POSITIONS

FORWARDS
LOOSEHEAD PROP - Typically a taller player and very quick out of the scrum. Normally the primary line-out jumper.

HOOKER - Very strong and powerful. Good over the ball and highly skilled.

TIGHTHEAD - Strongest player on the team, must be able to stabilize the right side of the scrum.

BACKS
SWEEPER - Very quick. Play maker and good one-on-one Defender.

1ST RECEIVER - Primary play maker, highly skilled, calm and visually aware of space.

CENTER - Good play maker. Very quick and good defender.

WING - Lots of speed, good finisher and defender.

In 7's rugby, teams have 5 reserves, preferably utility players with the ability to play more than one position.

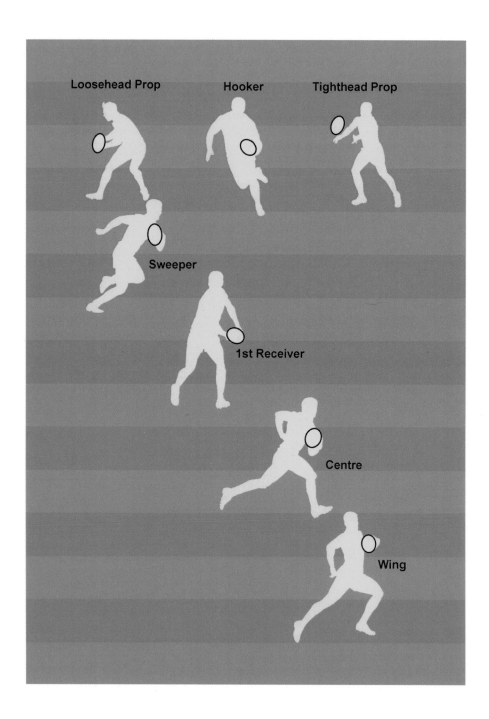

Loosehead Prop

Hooker

Tighthead Prop

Sweeper

1st Receiver

Centre

Wing

4. BALL HANDLING

The ability to catch and pass the ball with accuracy is essential in maintaining possession of the ball and manipulating defenders. As previously mentioned, the game of 7's is played on a regulation, full-size rugby field and, therefore, the width and distance of passes is increased by a massive measure. Players are often positioned at depth to give themselves enough time to complete the pass accurately. This width between players means that the angle and weight of each pass is varied all the time. Players need to have the skill set to make a variety of passes.

5. GAME PLAN - STRUCTURE - SHAPE

It's important to have a basic attacking shape to use. This provides players with clarity and also gives them the confidence they need to face high-pressure situations, as they have a default structure or shape to fall back on.

A very basic game plan is to always attempt to attack out wide because most teams defend with a sweeper covering behind them. There should always be space out wide because you can have 7 attackers on 6 defenders and 1 sweeper at the back.

Below are 3 simple examples of structures used attack:

1 Attack wide and set up a ruck to bring the ball back quick and penetrate through the middle or out wide again.

2 Attack to the middle of the field and attack same side or change direction.

3 Move the ball to the second last player on the open side whom makes a decision to either play to the outside and to bring it back with a late switch to create continuity to avoid the ruck and keep the ball alive, or the player changes direction to bring the ball to the other side before contact to create overlap on the opposite side of the field.

Essentially, an attack in 7s rugby is manipulating the defending players by moving the ball into open space back and forth until the defense can no longer cover enough space and ultimately lose connection, leading to a linebreak and potential try.

6. DEFENSE

It's important to understand that defense in 7's takes a lot of hard work, communication, and decision-making, as well as a high level of fitness. Defensively, teams need to have the ability to cover a lot of space and complete one-on-one tackles.

Players also need to be able to make difficult decisions, such as when to go for the steal, counter ruck, or stay on one's feet and defend the next phase.

The defense's main objective is to take time and space away from attackers to pressure them into making mistakes in order to get possession of the ball back.

Having line integrity and staying connected as a unit are of utmost importance for the defense, especially for beginner/youth 7's players who aren't able to take time and space away from their opponents because of their assortment of fitness levels, speed, and experience.

ACCURATE BALL PRESENTATION & CLEANER'S BODY POSITION

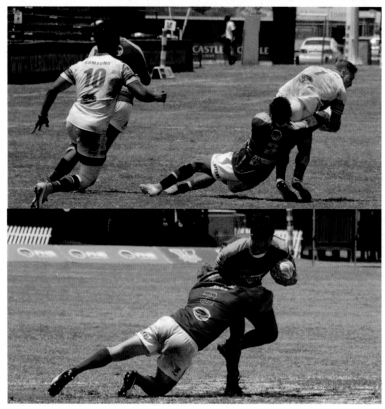

DEFENSIVE SET-UP FROM A SCRUM

SWEEPER POSITION IN GENERAL PLAY

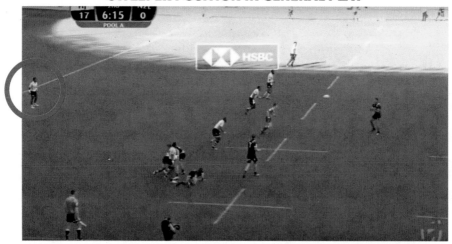

9

7. BREAKDOWN

The breakdown is one of the most important aspects of the attack as it is used to maintain possession and build phases. This puts the opposition under pressure and ultimately leads to tries being scored.

The breakdown can be broken down into 3 specific roles, namely:

BALL CARRIER: The player carrying the ball through the contact situation.

1   Ability to secure and protect the ball.

2   Works down to ground aggressively and gets behind the defender's feet to make the steal difficult for the tackler and the defending team.

3   Dynamically recoils their body and presents the ball accurately and efficiently towards their own team's side.

CLEANER: The player stabilizing the ruck and/or cleaning out the nearest potential threat. He/She needs to arrive quickly to the tackled ball carrier, maintaining a low and strong body of the player and ball on the ground.

SWEEPER: The player moving the ball away from the breakdown needs to react quickly and pass the ball as accurately and swiftly as possible.

ACCURATE BALL PRESENTATION AND CLEANER BODY POSITIONING

ACCURATE BALL PRESENTATION AND CLEANER BODY POSITIONING

GOOD PILFER BODY POSITIONING

8. PENALTIES/FREE KICKS

Your first option at penalty/free kick time is to play quickly and catch the defense offsides or play the clear and obvious space in front of you. Your second option is to aim to get the ball into open space as quickly as possible to get in behind the defensive line and score as soon as you can.

Thirdly, play a rehearsed-set penalty move with the specific aim of breaking through the opponents' line.

It is essential to put sufficient practice, time, and effort into this aspect of the game. If you can execute this phase well, you will have a good chance of winning the game, because there are a lot of penalties and free kicks in a sevens tournament.

9. FIRST PHASE

This aspect of the game is very important and is often the difference between losing games and winning tournaments, so in your coaching, ensure that this area of the game is well prepared.

9.1. SCRUM

The aim at scrum time is to get the ball out as quickly and effectively as possible, which in turn means that your scrum needs to be very steady and strong.

- The **LOOSEHEAD** prop needs to be low and aggressive as he must help steady the scrum.

- The **HOOKER** must understand how to hook the ball and still be able to scrum. On defense, he must always defends the blind side of the scrum.

- The **TIGHTHEAD** is most important on attack as he creates the overlap because of the right shoulder from the scrum and the fact that he is the strongest scrummager of the three.

Forward players must be able to play all three positions in the scrum because of the nature of Sevens tournaments.

PRE SCRUM SET UP

9.2. LINE-OUT

The purpose of the line-out is to get the play restarted after the ball has traveled over the line of touch (out of bounds). Try to keep this as simple and effective as possible.

- Normally, you want your Sweeper to throw the ball into the line-out as he also doubles around to pass the ball to the backline as the scrum half.

- Tallest players should be used as jumpers.

BELOW ARE A FEW EXAMPLES OF LINE-OUT OPTIONS:

OPTION 1: Bail out - the player in front of the line-out turns around and there is no jump. This is a low, hard throw at the player's hands, usually in front of his face.

OPTIONS 2: One-man lift - the player in the front of the line-out gets lifted by the player behind him.

OPTION 3: Two-man lift - the jumper in the middle of the line-out moves forward and takes it the ball at the front of the line-out. It is important that the back lifter remains ready and aware of when the jumper is ready to jump. This move is a quick, hard throw above the jumper's head.

OPTION 4: Two-man lift - the jumper will be in the middle of the line-out. Lifters will move and support the jumper to the middle of the line-out and lift the jumper when he decides the time is right to jump. This throw is more of a loop-throw over the front contesting pod.

OPTION 5: Two-man lift - the jumper in this scenario will move to the back of the line-out. Lifters will move with and support the jumper and lift him/her when they are ready to jump. This throw is a hard, flat throw in order to beat the contesting pod.

PRE LINE-OUT SET UP

TWO MAN LIFT

TWO MAN LIFT

POST LINE-OUT - SWEEPER RUNS AROUND TO RECEIVE BALL

9.3. KICK-OFFS

Kick-offs are certainly the most important set piece and the one that you need to spend the most time on in training because of the sheer amount of restarts in a 7's game as a result of many tries being scored.

There are many different setups a team can try for receiving a kick off.

Single-man lifts are very difficult to perfect but once mastered they can give you a big advantage for reclaiming the kickoffs because of the height your players would be able to produce.

In new/beginner teams whereby the players aren't able to get a lot of height on their restarts and are not as accurate, it is suggested to put 4 players up front spread across the width of the field along the 10m line and put 3 players about 10m behind the front 4, or visa versa, with 3 up front and 4 behind them. Coaches must ensure to put their best catchers of the ball in the positions most likely to be kicked on.

The drop kick itself is also very important. The more accurate the kick, the better you can plan and train strategies on how to reclaim possession of the ball off your own kickoff.

The main objective is to get possession from kickoffs or have a defensive strategy in place to get the possession back as soon after the kick as possible.

SINGLE MAN KICK OFF LIFT

PRE KICK OFF SET UP

KICK OFF CHASE

SINGLE MAN KICK OFF LIFT

9.4. PENALTY MOVES

Penalties happen all the time in 7s, so it's important to have accurate and effective starter moves in order to try and score right way without having to build phases.

The 1st and best option is to try to take the penalty tap as quick as possible to catch the defense offside or get a chance to attack against an unorganized defense.

2nd best option is to have a set of effective set plays. An important aspect to consider is to have certain players in certain positions when running a penalty move. Preferably, the Sweeper takes the penalty tap with two play makers on either side of him/her, two forwards next to them, and then two speedier players on the edges.

If the team can't score immediately, then the aim should be to create momentum and continuity on penalty moves. Insert 2 or 3 options based on the moves and perfect them. Make certain all of the team members understand their roles.

10. STARTER PLAYS OFF A SET PIECE

Divide your field into 3 channels-Wide, Middle, and Channel-closest to where the set piece takes place. Figure out which starter move would be most effective to use in each specific area. Keep the channel names similar to your lingo calls.

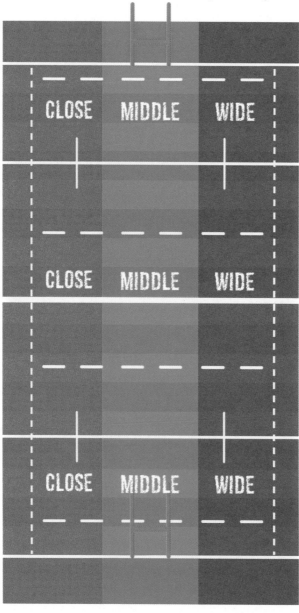

Always read from left to right - close, middle, and wide.

11. TEAM LINGO

Team lingo is very important for concise communication on the field in order to reach quick and effective decisions.

Create names for specific players and positions as this will also help with all of your coaching terminology.

Develop a specific theme for your team lingo, e.g. NATO codes, Golf, USA states, Music genres, etc.

Names are very important to use for basic memory.

SIMPLE EXAMPLES OF ATTACKING LINGO: (NATO THEME)
Pass the ball wide: Whiskey - (W for wide)
Change direction: Romeo - (R for reverse)
Taking contact: Delta - (D for direct)
Switch pass: Sierra - (S for switch)
Kick + chase: Kilo - (K for kick).

SIMPLE EXAMPLES OF DEFENSIVE LINGO:
Shadowing an overlap: Swim
Aggressive defense: Smash
1st player behind the ruck: Papa - (P for Pillar)
No contest at breakdown: Lima - (L for leave the ruck).

This is all up to the interpretation of the players, so be sure to choose lingo that is easy to memorize and is not too detailed or difficult to communicate on the field when a player is under fatigue and pressure.

Giving players fun positional names can be an entertaining and effective way of memorizing their roles in the team.

THE FOLLOWING ARE SIMPLE EXAMPLES FOR POSITIONAL NAMES:

FORWARDS

LOOSEHEAD PROP - Jumbo

HOOKER - Bullet

TIGHTHEAD - Rhino

BACKS

SWEEPER - Chicken

1ST RECEIVER - Pink Panther or PP

CENTRE - Rover

WING - Cheetah

12. KICKING

Kicking can be a very effective attacking weapon if all your players have the ability to execute a variety of different attacking kicks. Kickoffs and conversions are of course the most noteworthy kicks in the game of 7's and it's important that your primary kickers practice these kicks a lot so that they are accurate.

GRUBBER KICK: A grubber is a kick along the ground that is normally used when defenders are very close and almost committed to making a tackle. With the defensive lineup and space identified behind, the aim of this kick is to put behind the defensive line for your outside players to be able to chase and ultimately pick up the ball and score.

CHIP KICK: This kick is used when there is no sweeper defending behind the defensive line. It's a low kick in the air over a defender with the aim to regather the ball.

CROSS KICK: This kick is used from one side of the field to kick the ball to a teammate where there is lots of space or no defenders for them to gather and score points. This kick/move is often referred as a 'wiper' because of the shape of it, that of a windscreen wiper, moving from one side to another.

DROP KICK: It's important that this kick is always contestable with a lot of hang time so that the kicking team has the best possible chance of getting the ball back. The drop kick is also used to kick conversions-which are vital to matches-in which teams score the same amount of tries. Having an accurate kicker is integral to the success of a 7's team.

DROP- KICK CONVERSION

© Outsider Communications

13. TEAM CULTURE

It is essential to the success of any team that the correct set of values, culture, and team spirit are in place to ensure a team is mentally tough and resilient under pressure.

Below is a list of the most important components in establishing a strong team culture:

1   Set your team goals. Short, medium, and long-term.

2   Select a leadership group to drive a positive team culture through standards, ownership, and accountability with the guidance of the management.

3   Make certain that processes are put in place to deal with any situation within the team, disciplinary or otherwise.

4   Earning respect and building rapport with your players are also very important in driving a positive, high-performance team culture. Getting to know your players on a personal level will go a long way in times of struggle as a team. Always ask questions to ensure players are happy and are enjoying the experience. Encourage an open-door policy and have consistent one-on-ones with your players.

5   Keep referring back to your goals and values as a metric on which to base performance of the team, instead of just on results. If the emphasis is put in the process, the results will take care of themselves and long-term development will thrive. Encourage players to communicate honestly and productively without the fear of being called out. Deal with disappointment as a team.

14. STRENGTH AND CONDITIONING

It's important to incorporate fitness pockets into your training and strength sessions in order to best simulate a match-like scenario where skills are tested under fatigue. If possible, participating in weights sessions as a team is a great way to build character and team spirit amongst players.

Continuing on theme of match simulated fitness sessions. 7 Minute cardio sessions have proven to be extremely effective for fitness, particularly after a weights session and often with a 2 minute break in between rounds of 7 minutes, replicating that of a half-time during a match.

15. PRACTICE SESSION BREAKDOWN

The most important thing for each practice session is to have clear set of goals in mind based on the specific outcome you desire.

When coaching young players that are new to the sport, it is essential that your session is organized and includes lots of games that are both fun and productive.

Below is an example of a practice session breakdown (assuming two practices per week).

TIME		TRAINING	GROUP	Coach
Training Session 1				
Focus: Passing & Attack				
10 Min	Warm Up	Stand and Passing + progress		
		Dynamic Stretches (lower)		
		Passing Game		
		Dynamic Stretches (Upper B)		
Min	Skills Focus	Micro plays: - Switches, Skips, Overs & Unders etc.		
		4 on 3 & 5 on 4 plus 1		
		Off Load Game		
Fitness Pocket				
Min	Defence	Defence principles		
		Tackler		
		Roll out		
Min	Game Scenarios	Passing Ball with 7 on 7 with different level of pressure		
		Rucks on different part of the field.		
Min	Split	Forwards: Scrums & Kick Offs		
		Backs: Strike Moves & Kicking Attack		
Fitness Pocket				
Min	Game Plays From Set Pieces	Kick Offs		
		Scrums		
		Line Outs		
		Penalties		
		Different Type of Plays		

Training Session 2				
Focus: Contact & Defence				
TIME		**TRAINING**	**GROUP**	**Coach**
10 Min	Warm Up	Stand and Passing + progress		
		Dynamic Stretches (lower)		
		Passing Game (Contact)		
		Dynamic Stretches (Upper B)		
Min	Skills Focus	One on One tackling Drill		
		Tracking Drill		
		Post tackle roles		
Fitness Pocket				
Min	Defence	Defence principles		
		Tackler		
		4 on 3 & 5 on 4 plus 1		
Min	Game Scenarios	Passing Ball with 7 on 7 with different level of pressure		
		Rucks on different part of the field.		
Min	Split	Forwards: Line Outs & Kick Offs		
		Backs: Strike Moves & Kicking Attack		
Fitness Pocket				
Min	Plays	Kick Offs		
		Scrums		
		Line Outs		
		Penalties		
		Different Type of Plays		

CHARLIE PURDON

Charlie was born and raised in, 'rugby mad' South Africa and fell in love with the game when he began attending boarding school at a young age. Post schooling he has been fortunate to travel and partly make a career in rugby as a player, most recently in Southern California, USA. Charlie is passionate about the sport and considers himself a student of the game. He is currently the Director and Head Coach of a high performance Rugby Academy in San Diego, focusing on fundamental skill development. He also plays his own rugby for Old Mission Beach Athletic Club in the Pacific Rugby Premiership.

IAN CAMPBELL-McGEACHY

Ian is a very well-established 7's coach based in Stellenbosch, South Africa. He has served as the Stellenbosch University 7's coach for the past 6 years, winning the National Championship in 4 of them. His role also included head of skills development at 'Maties' - the biggest rugby club in the world, with over 1300 registered players. He has assisted the Western Province 7's team, although his greatest achievement is being named Head Coach of the South African Students team that competed in the World Student Games in Russia in 2013. Ian or 'Miyagi' as he's better known, has become an icon in this student town, and his passion for, and devotion to his players is evidence of this. His philosophy is fashioned by a positive learning environment built on skills and sheer enjoyment of the game and all it encompasses.

Made in the USA
Coppell, TX
31 December 2022

10142523R00024